Dirty Dishes:
Every Woman Has Them

By
Adrienne Latrise Draper

~adrienneldraper.com~

Dirty Dishes: Every Woman Has Them

January 2013

COPYRIGHT © 2013 Adrienne Latrise Draper

ALL RIGHTS RESERVED. This book contains material protected under International and Federal Copyright Laws and Treaties. Any unauthorized reprint or use of this material is prohibited. No part of this book may be reproduced or transmitted in any form or by any means, electronic or mechanical, including photocopying, recording, or by any information storage and retrieval system without express written permission from the author/publisher.

Cover photo courtesy of Christopher Draper.

Published in the United States by Adrienne Latrise Draper
Edited by Aja La'Starr®

The Library of Congress has a record of this publication.

Printed in the United States of America

ISBN-13: 978-1481846110

Dirty Dishes: Every Woman Has Them

Dedication:

I would like to dedicate this book to women of all ages throughout the world; because I believe that we all have something in common: *imperfections (or dirty dishes)*. This book allows you to identify with at least one of the examples of how we all have dirty dishes in our lives.

There are many women throughout my life- from relatives to strangers-who have inspired me to write this book. Through their experiences, as well as my own, I was able to create a book that highlights occurrences that we at times fail to discuss.

It is my greatest desire that each woman who read this book is inspired in some way; if after reading this book, you can identify with your own dirty dishes-then my writing has not been in vain.

If you are a woman who has already cleaned up her kitchen, I hope that you will use your experiences and this book to teach another woman what to do with her dirty dishes.

Dirty Dishes: Every Woman Has Them

Dirty Dishes:

Introduction

Dirty Dishes

- Sink Full Of Dishes
- Can't Take The Heat, Get Out The Kitchen
- I Need A Better Kitchen
- I Only Like His Cooking
- Side Dish
- Paper Plate
- But He Loves My Cooking
- Should I Order Take Out
- How Long Will You Let Your Dishes Soak

Broken Dishes

- My Biscuits Are Burning
- Dishing Out
- It's Not Polite To Talk And Chew
- Keena's Deadly Recipe
- Fruit Dries Up
- Washing Dishes in Dirty Water
- Aluminum In The Microwave
- Addicted To The Flavor
- Everything Can't Be Slow Cooked

Who's Washing Your Dishes?

- Full Course Meal
- Who's Recipe Are You Using
- Bad Cooks, Cook Bad
- Who's Cooking In Your Kitchen
- Should I Try This Dish
- Mothers Are The Best Cooks
- Teaching Mama How To Cook
- Fine China

How To Clean Your Dishes

- Preheat Your Stove
- Change The Temperature
- Cook In Your Own Kitchen

Introduction

No one likes dirty dishes-but as women; we have all had dirty dishes at some point in our lives. Dirty dishes are those abusive relationships, identity conflicts, spiritual-warfares, or any form of rejection that have cluttered and in some cases destroyed our very existence.

Just about every woman that I know, even the most accomplished women-has had-or currently, has dirty dishes. And though their strength and power radiates the very fiber of their being, there is no question that their ability to overcome life's obstacles happened the exact moment they began washing those dirty dishes.

One of the main issues with having dirty dishes is not realizing that you have them. Many women walk around blinded by their own ignorance and insecurities and pay more attention to someone else's dirty dishes rather than their own. While they can point out how unclean someone else's dishes are-theirs are left soaking in the sink. However, it is very important to recognize the urgency of cleaning your dishes and cleaning them thoroughly. By letting dirty dishes soak, it creates a stench, or a foul odor that can make living life/dealing with others unbearable.

But the moment that we as women realize that our dirty dishes are the reason we are not progressing, and the reason we are not succeeding, is the moment we will be liberated from our current situation. Therefore, I encourage every woman to acknowledge your dirty dishes, to clean your dirty dishes and to do everything necessary to ensure that your sink is free from dirty dishes.

Dirty Dishes: Every Woman Has Them

My Promise

I promise to open my mind, my heart, my spirit and my soul to wholeheartedly receive the messages in ***Dirty Dishes.***

Your name

Adrienne Latrise Draper

Adrienne Latrise Draper

Dirty Dishes: Every Woman Has Them

Do not attempt to do a thing unless you are sure of yourself; but do not relinquish it simply because someone else is not sure of you.

~Stewart E. White~

Dirty Dishes: Every Woman Has Them

Chapter 1: Dirty Dishes

Sometimes, the most significant people in your life simply do not understand the plans that God has for you; therefore, seldom do they offer their approval for your achievements and accolades throughout life. In those instances, when their approval and appreciation are all that seem to matter to you-you run the risk of your dreams going unfulfilled and your goals unaccomplished.

As you would expect, everyone needs support; and furthermore, it is extremely vital that you find others who are just as enthused and compassionate about your endeavors as you are. But I do encourage you to not waste any time worrying about people who do not endorse your dreams; because anytime you wait for the stamp of approval from those who do not share your vision- that is time that you could be using to perfect your craft or invest in yourself.

Over the years, I have been fortunate enough to acquire many great friends and colleagues with whom I've extended much support and praise to for the great things they have accomplished. But no one has received as much of my support as my older sister. Realizing that we both have similar talents and abilities, we have always optimistically uplifted and sustained one another. To this day, we are constantly pushing each other towards recognizing and utilizing our greatest potential.

On the contrary, I know a wealth of people whose need for approval is so crucial that it actually plays a huge role in their survival. In fact, other people make every decision in their lives, because they lack the confidence to make the right choices.

When I was in college, I knew a young lady who

Dirty Dishes: Every Woman Has Them

was so obsessed with being accepted by others that she continually altered her appearance to appease her peers. There was an instance when she wore a certain dress that some upperclassmen girls did not like so she took it off. When I asked her why she decided to change, she admitted that it was because of the upperclassmen's disdain for her dress. Out of curiosity, I asked her when she goes shopping, does she purchase items that she likes or that other people like. A bit puzzled, she replied that the items she purchases are items that she likes. So naturally, my question to her was, "if the things that you purchase for yourself are items that you like, why would the opinions of others matter so much to you?"

Over the course of my life, I have always been rather eccentric and outgoing; and when it comes to my appearance-my family and close friends never know what to expect from me from day to day. I am constantly changing and reinventing myself.

One day I may wear a wig, the next day a weave ponytail, an Afro or even braids depending on my mood for the day. In my daily efforts of being the best me that I can be- I am constantly reminded of a great message my friend Basamba Sao shared with me, "It is not your business what people think of you." People say all the time that they do not care what others may think of them-but the truth is many people are so desperate for validation that their need for approval actually consumes their lives.

More often than not, the persons who cause us the most pain are those who are closest to us. In my life, my loved ones had the greatest effect on my decisions and me. If I expressed an interest in something, they would shut it down. However, if I told a complete stranger the same thing, their opinion was useless to me because I believed my loved ones were looking out for my best interests. It took me going through a lot of things to realize I was only operating for other people. I finally got to a point where I questioned, "What am I doing for myself? How was I insuring my own happiness?" After constantly asking myself those questions, I realized that I no longer existed, because who I had become was a fabricated version of my true self.

Dirty Dishes: Every Woman Has Them

Can you recall a time when someone said/did something offensive you? State who that person is and explain how you felt in that moment.

Dirty Dishes: Every Woman Has Them

What are you pursuing right now? What are some barriers that may be preventing you from accomplishing your pursuits?

_____
_____
_____
_____
_____
_____
_____
_____
_____
_____
_____
_____
_____
_____
_____

Dirty Dishes: Every Woman Has Them

Is there anyone who has discouraged you in your efforts to pursue your goals? State their name and discuss their effect on your life.

_____
_____
_____
_____
_____
_____
_____
_____
_____
_____
_____
_____
_____
_____
_____
_____
_____
_____
_____
_____

Dirty Dishes: Every Woman Has Them

Why do you believe their opinion matters?

Dirty Dishes: Every Woman Has Them

What will it take for you to continue pursuing your endeavors even if others never approves of it?

_____
_____
_____
_____
_____
_____
_____
_____
_____
_____
_____
_____
_____
_____
_____
_____
_____
_____

Dirty Dishes: Every Woman Has Them

Dirty Dishes: Every Woman Has Them

"The defects of the children mirror the defects of their parents."

~Herbert Spencer~

Dirty Dishes: Every Woman Has Them

Sink full of Dishes

I was very fortunate to be raised in a loving and supportive household. My mother always did her best to provide the most stable lifestyle for my siblings and me; and even though her relationship with my stepfather did not last-when they were together, he also served as a great example to us.

My mother and stepfather were so family-oriented, that we grew up being exposed to distant relatives and loved ones all over the country. We travelled down south regularly; and annual family reunions were as common to us, as going to school each day. I often reflect on the way I was raised and use past experiences from my upbringing in my own motherhood journey.

My parents really showed us what love looked like. Even old pictures of the two of them display their true love through their smiles and affection for one another.

But sadly, some people were not as fortunate as me. Perhaps you grew up feeling unloved and unwanted. Maybe you are a woman who has been molested or violated in some way. Possibly, one or both of your parents abandoned you. When you grow up without the inherent love from your parents, living life can be like having a sink full of dishes. You may acquire piles and piles of issues that prevent you from experiencing a fruitful life.

True enough, some parents do an awful job raising their children with love and respect; but the essential values you lack from your parents will definitely affect your friendships and relationships with others. I know women who only attract aggressively vulgar men, like the men their mothers dated. I know lesbian women who demonstrate male characteristics trying to be the father they never had. And sadly, some women accept mediocre

Dirty Dishes: Every Woman Has Them

relationships because they are clueless as to what a potential mate should be like to them.

There are a number of men who see our vulnerabilities and prey on them. But you must evaluate your own life and determine what your happiness will look like. Sometimes, being honest with ourselves is the most difficult thing to do. It may be difficult accepting that our relationships with our parents transpire into how we have learned to adapt to other people. If your parent wasn't trustworthy, it's common for you to have trust issues; but if your parents celebrated your every accomplishment, you will more than likely know and own your self-worth and treat people with compassion.

The older I become, the more I realize I have the power to establish healthy relationships with others. It's not fair to our mates to overcompensate for our emptiness as well as cheat them out of being trustworthy, loving and supportive towards us.

So I implore to you, how long do you plan to leave your house with a sink full of dishes? Imagine how liberated you will feel once you begin washing and putting those dishes away. Within your friendships and relationships, it means recognizing your issues, dealing with your issues and making certain that those issues do not continue to consume your life.

Dirty Dishes: Every Woman Has Them

Describe your relationship with your parents? Could it be improved?

_____
_____
_____
_____
_____
_____
_____
_____
_____
_____
_____
_____
_____
_____
_____
_____
_____

Dirty Dishes: Every Woman Has Them

Does the way that you were raised have a negative or positive affect on the way you handle issues in your life? (Describe in detail)

_____
_____
_____
_____
_____
_____
_____
_____
_____
_____
_____
_____
_____
_____
_____
_____
_____
_____
_____

Dirty Dishes: Every Woman Has Them

Are there any areas in your life that feels like a sink full of dishes? If so, discuss here; then think of some ways you can begin to wash them?

Dirty Dishes: Every Woman Has Them

"Never grow a wishbone, where your backbone ought to be."

~Clementine Paddleford~

Dirty Dishes: Every Woman Has Them

Can't Take the Heat, Get Out the Kitchen!

Throughout my life, I have encountered a number of women who found pleasure in passing judgment and belittling other people. I've seen these women treat their spouses and loved ones with nothing but cruelty and vindictiveness. These women are usually very defensive and have really nasty attitudes; and they do not rest easy if they cannot ridicule, criticize or demean people around them. They disguise their pain with a false sense of power and use their energy to point out the flaws and insecurities of others. I call these women *Anticipators*; they anticipate admiration or anything they can receive from others.

Admiration Anticipators seeks admiration and always waits for people to be in awe of what they have or what they've done. They want you to look up to them because of their possessions and usually have superficial confidence and poor social skills. Behind all of their cockiness are insecurities and loneliness. It doesn't matter that they keep an immaculate home, or cook edible meals because people that are close to them, dread being around them. Typically, *Admiration Anticipators* always think that they are right and others are wrong; and even in the cases where they are proven wrong-others will apologize to them to keep tensions down.

Receiving Anticipators, seek whatever others have to offer them-and most times, they are not givers themselves. They're hand is always open to receive because they feel they're entitled to something. For some reason, these women happen to have men in their lives; but if their spouses have children, she's definitely nasty towards his children or his family. *Receiving Anticipators* make everyone around them uncomfortable and usually their home is very unwelcoming. If her mate is family-

Dirty Dishes: Every Woman Has Them

oriented, she makes it very difficult for him to balance between pleasing his family and satisfying her.

With both anticipators, they can dish it out but they can't take it in. If they feel as if they're losing the argument or someone isn't bending their way, they lose it. The *Admiration Anticipator* will leave a heated argument or hang up the call before ever admitting fault or guilt; however, it will take the *Receiving Anticipator* to have people cut her off or her mate leaving her, before she breaks down and reconsider her ways.

If you are an *Anticipator* you need to really examine the underline problem behind your stance; sometimes, you may find that the reason behind your pain dates all the way back to your childhood. Take a moment to think about how your actions affect those around you. How do you think you would feel if you were on the opposite end of your ridicule?

If you know you would not be able to withstand the heat, then perhaps you should get out of the kitchen-and really make strides in changing your ways.

Dirty Dishes: Every Woman Has Them

After reading about the two types of Anticipators, do you feel that you have similar characteristics? If so, how do you plan to address it? If not, do you know of anyone who falls into that category? Describe how you feel when you are around them.

_____

_____

_____

_____

_____

_____

_____

_____

_____

_____

_____

_____

_____

_____

_____

Dirty Dishes: Every Woman Has Them

How do you think your family and friends perceive your character? If you don't know, take a moment and ask them. Use this space to talk about how you believe others view you on a day-to-day basis.

Dirty Dishes: Every Woman Has Them

Dirty Dishes: Every Woman Has Them

"One bird in the hand is more valuable than two in the woods."

~African Proverb~

I Need A Better Kitchen!

Kim always desired the best that life had to offer. She was constantly investing in things she felt would validate her self-worth. She indulged in many "Get Rich Quick" schemes and pyramids-which only granted her temporary gratification.

She was a beautiful, educated woman with poise and zest who lacked stability. She was great at selling herself, but it never took long for others to see how superficial she really was. She was chasing the idea of being rich, but never prepared herself for if it were to ever happen.

I heard a sermon years ago, that reminded me of Kim's situation; the minister talked about how we want better things, but are we taking good care of the things we have now? Often times, we look at the success and blessings of others and feel entitled to the same rewards. But have we worked as hard to acquire those things? More importantly, do we know what others went through to get what they have?

I am a strong believer that what is for me, is for me; and what is for you is for you. And whenever God is ready to bless me with a bigger home-I'll prepare myself to move. Otherwise, until I hear God speak to me, I will humbly embrace the home where I currently reside.

There is a parable in the bible (Matthew 25:15) that talks about a master who left three slaves with his money. Two slaves were able to double their money while the other slave hid his in the ground. The two slaves who doubled their money were made rulers while the other one was cast away to darkness.

You never know if God is trying to prepare you for something better; but if you are constantly wasting energy

Dirty Dishes: Every Woman Has Them

being envious of others and their things, you run the risk of missing out on the wonderful things designed specifically for you.

Women like Kim are **Chasers**: people who are generally running from something and have a tendency to not be satisfied with self. When you are a chaser, you try so hard to live up to standards and expectations that are sometimes unattainable. **Chasers** fear judgment from the very ones that they value endorsement from. **Chasers** are always trying to keep up with the Jones'-which can be extremely strenuous.

However, staying true to yourself and listening to God can open the door to overflow and abundance in your life. Stop complaining about wanting a new kitchen-and learn how to beautify the one you already have.

****

Repeat these words 3x a day until you believe it:

I am secure and satisfied with the woman I am. My talents and abilities are enough to sustain me. I am destined for greatness!

****

Dirty Dishes: Every Woman Has Them

Have you ever desired something greatly, and questioned why you could not seem to obtain it? What was it, and why do you feel you could not get it at the time?

_____
_____
_____
_____
_____
_____
_____
_____
_____
_____
_____
_____
_____
_____
_____

Dirty Dishes: Every Woman Has Them

"Love, the poet said, is woman's whole existence"
~Virgina Woolf~

I Only Like His Cooking!

Mariah was so in love with Stan that her world literally revolved around him. While most people wrote him off, she praised him because she always saw his true potential. Anytime Stan was in a bind, Mariah was always right there to bail him out.

Due to his criminal lifestyle, Stan was constantly in and out of jail; and whenever he was away, Mariah felt very lonely and stressed. But when he returned, it was like a light was ignited between them and everything was perfect. She was happiest with him. She literally worshipped the ground he walked on. Stan was her heaven on earth, but like anything that seems too good to be true- their paths, eventually took a turn for the worst.

Stan left Mariah, and it was as if he took her air supply with him. She became very depressed and suffered many negative effects of a broken heart. She had lost her appetite, her drive and any ambition to move on. Mariah never physically recovered because she loved hard.

Sometimes, we as women like to sample other dishes to satisfy our carnal cravings. But there are those women who only prefer one type of dish, prepared by the same chef. Mariah felt like she could only be fulfilled by eating what Stan cooked; despite his burnt and overcooked dishes-whatever he prepare she accepted with grace.

We have to realize that in everything there is variety; don't be so invested in one type of dish that you begin to settle for a foul taste. If a dish is not edible to your body, then perhaps it is time for you to consider a different chef.

Dirty Dishes: Every Woman Has Them

Dirty Dishes: Every Woman Has Them

Dirty Dishes: Every Woman Has Them

"Every wise woman buildeth her house: but the foolish plucketh it down with her hands."

Proverbs 14:1

Dirty Dishes: Every Woman Has Them

Side Dish

So many women have convinced themselves that they are fine with being the other woman. They tell themselves, "I'll be that other woman; as long as I'm the only other woman." These women tend to lavish themselves in the perks of being a mistress. They enjoy the gifts, quality time and the intimacy with no attachments. But as time progresses, those same women will learn that it is not so desirable to be the side dish.

When a man has a hearty meal in front of him, having a side dish is just an added bonus. How many men do you know that actually marry their mistresses? Mistresses may think that the ball in is in their court, but no one really benefits from affairs. The sexual risks become increasingly dangerous; the emotional baggage starts weighing down on you; all while some selfish man is going back and forth between women with no regard to their well-being.

Typically, if/when a man becomes separated from his main woman-he finds refuge in the other woman (the side dish). But becoming the main entrée after being a side dish only makes room for more side dishes to catch his attention when things go sour with you. He may start to reflect on what he lost and impose his misery onto you. That same fun guy who took his side dish to all the concerts and restaurants is now tight with every dime since assets are being split down the middle with his former wife. If you're honest with yourself- you know you don't want a piece of a man. Because remember, if he was bold enough to be unfaithful to the woman before you; chances are he will do the same thing to you.

Dirty Dishes: Every Woman Has Them

"Family values are a little like family vacations--subject to changeable weather and remembered more fondly with the passage of time. Though it rained all week at the beach, it's often the momentary rainbows that we remember."
~Leslie Dreyfous~

Paper Plates

Have you ever met a woman who saves her paper plates and plastic utensils? She even washes them with plans to reuse them again. What she fails to realize is that those dishes aren't meant to be used over and over again; but for some reason she just keeps holding on to them.

Just about everyone has found it hard to let something go; it's like you continue to hold on to it knowing that its condition isn't strong enough to endure.

I've had many experiences where I had to make a choice of whether to keep holding on to the pain of something, or to accept that it happened and heal from it. Especially regarding relationships; we want to keep holding on to someone who was only supposed to be around long enough for us to learn from the experience.

Sometimes, we push others aside to create space for those who were not destined for our journeys. Make the decision now, are you going to spend 7 more: minutes, days, months or years in the mist of it or are you going to take steps towards healing from it? Because remember, it was a paper plate-you deserve the real thing!

Dirty Dishes: Every Woman Has Them

"When we are not in love too much, we are not in love enough."

~Bussy Rabutin~

Dirty Dishes: Every Woman Has Them

But He Loves My Cooking!

There are many women in today's society who accept mediocrity in relationships because they think they are so in love. They accept verbal, physical and mental abuse at the hands of the very ones who claim to love them so much. But the idea that love is the only element necessary to make a relationship flourish is a strong misconception; it is like saying you only need flour to bake a cake. With any delicious and hearty meal, there are key ingredients that are mixed together to create it.

Similarly, relationships take a lot of work in order to experience longevity; but if both parties are not equally invested in the future of the union, perhaps it is time to re-evaluate the status of the relationship. I know many married women who are currently living as single parents because their husbands refuse to help with the children or around the house. His off days at work are "his days off" so his wife does not expect him to do anything. Other relatives attend his children's special events while he rarely makes time for them at all. But when dinnertime comes around, he expects to eat; despite the fact that his wife has a career as well, in addition to being the primary caregiver for their children.

We have to realize, being a woman is a multi-faceted job. We are natural caregivers, educators, nurturers etc. and over time, we have become masters at the same duties as our male counterparts. How many housewives have you seen do the job of many but get little to no compensation? How many relationships have you seen where a woman is being controlled and manipulated and her every moved is calculated by her mate?

"But He Loves My Cooking," some women proudly exclaims. But as women, we can tend to be blinded by the obvious signs in front of us. While it may be flattering that

Dirty Dishes: Every Woman Has Them

your mate loves your cooking, how often do they cook for you? How often do they offer to help you to cook? The more you don't require the basic necessities from your mate, they more you won't receive them. If it means asking your mate to help prepare a meal, or designate days where they take the children to the park-you have to be proactive in your relationship. Otherwise, you will be stuck trying to figure out how things went terribly wrong.

Dirty Dishes: Every Woman Has Them

Do you feel that "love" is enough to sustain a relationship? Why or why not?

_____
_____
_____
_____
_____
_____
_____
_____
_____
_____
_____
_____
_____
_____
_____
_____
_____

Dirty Dishes: Every Woman Has Them

What are some other elements needed to make a relationship thrive?

_____

_____

_____

_____

_____

_____

_____

_____

_____

_____

_____

_____

_____

_____

_____

_____

_____

Dirty Dishes: Every Woman Has Them

What are some of the major challenges women face within relationships? In your opinion, what are some ways they can overcome those challenges?

_____

_____

_____

_____

_____

_____

_____

_____

_____

_____

_____

_____

_____

_____

_____

Dirty Dishes: Every Woman Has Them

The heart knows it's own bitterness, and no stranger shares its joy

Proverbs 14:10

Dirty Dishes: Every Woman Has Them

Should I Order Take Out

When a man cheats, it's most likely with someone he hasn't already been with; where as some women will revert back to a past relationship or entertain someone who's often opposite of their mate. Most women who cheat aren't boasting or bragging about it because it isn't something they want to leak. Women can be so discreet even their loved ones are clueless of their infidelity.

Usually women who leave clues of their infidelity are involved with men who are laid back. It's typical for them to enjoy the ride and believe they don't care if their spouse stays or goes. What they fail to acknowledge is their mister (male name for mistress) isn't going to be fully committed and that laidback man could move on. The reality is, men have a greater chance of finding happiness with another woman faster than women. It doesn't matter how beautiful you are, you can meet someone else, but sometimes it takes a few relationships later to find stability again.

Middle-aged married woman are playing Russian Roulette because the security of years invested in a marriage, adult children and grandchildren now being split into two households leaves emotional scars on all involved. With men, Viagra has played its part in divorce as well as women undergoing plastic surgery or extreme weight loss. Their confidence is heightened, so the sexual attention from others becomes open court. If you are one of these women ask yourself: Should I order take out or continue to create edible meals in my own kitchen to satisfy my appetite?

Dirty Dishes: Every Woman Has Them

If you have already committed to leaving or he has left ask yourself:

Am I happier now or is there still a void? If so Why?

_____
_____
_____
_____
_____
_____
_____
_____
_____
_____
_____
_____
_____
_____

Dirty Dishes: Every Woman Has Them

Dirty Dishes: Every Woman Has Them

"The road of by and by, leads to the house of never."
~Old Spanish saying~

Dirty Dishes: Every Woman Has Them

How Long Will You Let Your Dishes Soak?

Everyone knows someone who is really talented but never seems to go anywhere with their gifts. In dealing with these people, perhaps you have questioned, "Why can't they seem to get it together?" These people are considered *Dreamers*, a person who aspires to use their abilities but don't trust their own potential to do so. They have the potential and the means to make it happen, but just won't follow their dreams.

In a lot of cases, *Dreamers* have *Enablers*, people who believe in dreamers and are just as passionate about their ambitions as they are. But ***Dreamers who just don't seem to take their gifts and abilities seriously gradually disappoint Enablers.*** In some cases, it takes a *Dreamer* to cross an *Enabler* for an enabler to step back and allow the dreamer to take charge of their own lives.

Over the years, I came to understand that I was a *Dreamer*. I'm not sure if it was inherited, but I started noticing that I was constantly talking about what I wanted to do, but made every excuse not to do it. Fear was the root of my procrastination. There was a time when I felt others would not take me seriously if I pursued my dreams without a degree; but when I received my Bachelor's degree my new excuse was my family. I had to come to the conclusion that, if I kept making excuses, I would never see the rewards of stepping out on faith.

Being a *Dreamer* is like eating a good meal, taking the dirty dishes to the sink and letting them soak. How long will you let days turn to weeks, to months, to years before you decide that it is crucial to wash those dishes? Find the courage to stand firm and no longer allow fear to linger in your life. If you are an *Enabler*, don't continue to help someone pursue his or her dream while yours becomes

Dirty Dishes: Every Woman Has Them

deferred. As an ***Enabler***, you become like the crude on someone else's dish that's causing them to soak longer.

We all have reasons why we shouldn't and not enough reasons why we should. Re-evaluate your life and figure out why you've been letting your dishes soak so long and get in the mode of cleaning them.

Dirty Dishes: Every Woman Has Them

In your opinion, what are some of the major problems with being a dreamer?

Dirty Dishes: Every Woman Has Them

In your opinion, what are some of the major problems with being an enabler?

_____
_____
_____
_____
_____
_____
_____
_____
_____
_____
_____
_____
_____
_____
_____
_____
_____
_____
_____
_____

Dirty Dishes: Every Woman Has Them

What can enablers do to help dreamers achieve their goals?

Dirty Dishes: Every Woman Has Them

Why do you believe you are so important?
(Really think about the question before answering)

_____
_____
_____
_____
_____
_____
_____
_____
_____
_____
_____
_____
_____
_____
_____
_____
_____
_____
_____
_____

Dirty Dishes: Every Woman Has Them

What are some of the triggers you have when interacting with others?

_____
_____
_____
_____
_____
_____
_____
_____
_____
_____
_____
_____
_____
_____

Dirty Dishes: Every Woman Has Them

Fill in the sentence:

1. In order that I have a healthy relationship with

   _____
   (State the person's name)

   I will do my best to acknowledge how I speak to them.

2. I will allow my relationship with my mate to be separate from the relationship he/she has with their family. I will not interfere when he/she assists

   _____
   (State the person's name)

3. I will learn how to be more respectful to

   _____
   (State the person's name)

4. My importance is not determined by my

   _____
   (State the possession)

*After carefully filling in everything, recite it back and own it!

Dirty Dishes: Every Woman Has Them

Dirty Dishes: Every Woman Has Them

"No sun will shine in my day today. The high yellow moon won't come out to play. Darkness has covered my light and has changed my day into night...where is this love, to be found?"

~Bob Marley~

Chapter 2: Broken Dishes

Have you ever felt the intensity from a dish breaking? Have you even been cut by a piece of broken glass? Has someone ever thrown a plate or a bowl at your head in a heated argument? It is no question that broken dishes are undesirable; and more than likely, they are nearly impossible to mend. Broken dishes in our lives are like the devastation we experience due to different forms of abuse.

Many women experience abuse on a day to day basis-and it is important to note, that abuse in not only physical; abuse can also be *mental*, *emotional*, *spiritual*, and *verbal*.

When experiencing abuse, sometimes it is not easy to talk about it because of the shame and embarrassment attached. And in many cases, the abused person feels as though they provoked the abuser-ultimately, causing the abuse.

Domestic Violence in today's society is becoming more and more common; so common, that even children are beginning to mimic the abuse they see at the hands of their parents and their peers. Abuse can literally make time stand still; but when it goes undetected or untreated, things can really begin to spiral out of control in your life.

Years ago, I was jumped by three girls as I tried to defend my younger cousin from a few bullies in her apartment complex. By the time the attack was over, apparently, I had been dragged nearly four cars down from where I was parked and my two year-old son remained

Dirty Dishes: Every Woman Has Them

strapped in his car seat. One of the effects from that attack was paranoia.

Ironically, I began accepting various forms of abuse from others because I felt helpless and vulnerable as a result of the attack. Eventually, I neglected my own life. But one day, I decided I would face my fears and deal with what I had tried to conceal for years. I had become everything, to everyone, but myself. I had to center myself and focus on growing spiritually; so that in connecting with God-it would be easier for me to overcome my personal fears.

I felt liberated! I had been in a dark place for so long and it was time for me to come out of whatever it was that kept me trapped. I had to face a lot of things that I had put on the back burner; and it was time for me to wash all of the dirty dishes I left to soak. It was time for me to fulfill new endeavors and make the ones I've talked about for years, a reality.

Sometimes, we give people permission to abuse us. People see us being so hard on ourselves that they feel comfortable adding to our self-degradation. Even when we are presented with a normal, healthy relationship; we begin to sabotage the relationship because we feel unworthy of being truly loved.

I encourage women to take a step back and look at your broken dishes. You must understand that in some cases, it is not about trying to restore what you've lost; but maybe it is time to accept that those broken dishes are of no more use to you-and it is time to invest in better dishes.

Dirty Dishes: Every Woman Has Them

Abuse comes in many forms (physical, verbal, emotional, mental, spiritual, etc.) how has abuse affected your life? Have you been abused? Have you abused someone? Discuss here.

Dirty Dishes: Every Woman Has Them

Do you have any "broken dishes" in your kitchen right now? In other words, are there some issues or challenges you are currently facing that are a barrier in your life?

_____
_____
_____
_____
_____
_____
_____
_____
_____
_____
_____
_____
_____
_____
_____
_____
_____

Dirty Dishes: Every Woman Has Them

Dirty Dishes: Every Woman Has Them

"Setbacks are setups for testimonies."
~T.D. Jakes~

Dirty Dishes: Every Woman Has Them

My Biscuits Are Burning!

Sandy was a hard worker; she was punctual, dependable, thorough and friendly. She had been on her job for fifteen years then boom... a layoff. Before she knew it, she had been laid off for two years and her savings had virtually depleted. With few options, she decided to move in with her sister Linda until she could afford to live on her own again.

But moving in with her sister was one of the worst mistakes she had ever made. Even though she paid rent, her sister took advantage of her situation and treated her like a child. Sandy had no privacy and felt obligated to do odd things for her sister simply because she was living under her roof. Linda constantly reminded Sandy about everything she was doing to help her get on her feet-which ultimately made Sandy feel helpless, vulnerable and worthless.

During those moments of desperation and defenselessness, you must understand that your setbacks are just setups for your testimonies. I recall a sermon preached by Bishop T.D. Jakes about how most successful battles are won using strange weapons (Sampson-jaw bone of an ass, David-a rag and a rock, etc.), so you never know if your uncomfortable situation was purposely created so that you can witness God turn impossibilities into promising victories in your life. You must trust that God will not only create your path, but he will direct it.

An ordinary person wouldn't know what to do with a rag and a rock if Goliath were coming their way, but when you have faith you know God has prepared you for your battle. I once heard that faith is like pictures developed in the dark. God will make your voice heard and your presence visible.

It wasn't long before Sandy saved enough money,

Dirty Dishes: Every Woman Has Them

got a steady job again and moved out. But before moving forward, she created an execution plan that would help her to avoid reliving the same setback.

There are many things that can happen to us throughout life to cause us to be in a similar situation as Sandy-so it is vitally important to stay spiritually grounded and focused to ensure you can handle whatever comes your way.

The next time you put your biscuits in the oven (or experience a situation beyond your control), be sure to stay in the kitchen and take the necessary actions to ensure your biscuits don't burn next time.

Dirty Dishes: Every Woman Has Them

When setting goals, it is essential to have a Plan A, Plan B and sometimes a Plan C. Have you ever failed to have a back-up plan; what happened as a result?

_____
_____
_____
_____
_____
_____
_____
_____
_____
_____
_____
_____
_____
_____
_____
_____

Dirty Dishes: Every Woman Has Them

Are you currently working to achieve a certain goal? If so, list your Plan A, Plan B and Plan C here. If you are really ambitious, list a Plan D.

Plan A:
_____
_____
_____
_____
_____

Plan B:
_____
_____
_____
_____
_____

Plan C:
_____
_____
_____
_____
_____

Plan D:
_____
_____
_____
_____

Dirty Dishes: Every Woman Has Them

Dirty Dishes: Every Woman Has Them

"Gossip, it's the mother's milk of journalism."
~Herb Caen~

Dirty Dishes: Every Woman Has Them

Dishing Out!

Sarah always despised living in a glass house; even though her mother worked tirelessly to provide a stable, loving home for her and her brother Bobby-things were not always as good as they had seemed. On the outside looking in-Sarah's friends thought she had the coolest mother ever. Her mother was outgoing, lively and had a very animated personality. Her friends could not get enough of the embarrassing stories her mother shared with them and anyone else in listening range.

But Sarah's mother had a tendency to go too far. She would share intimate experiences that were not meant to be repeated. And over time, Sarah and her brother became very rebellious as a result of their mother's disregard of their feelings. Although it may not have been her intentions, their mother's constant need to have others laugh at their expense caused many problems within their relationship.

When Sarah became an adult, she resented her mother; and found it very difficult to confide in her in fear that she would use her personal trials as the bunt of her jokes.

Sarah's mother shared so much of their personal family business that even her mother's co-workers felt the need to criticize and offer their opinions. Over time, her mother's persistent gossiping forged a huge gap between them. The fact that Sarah's proudest moments were not celebrated by her mother-perhaps because there was no drama-was very upsetting.

As women we have to be very careful with what we say about people. Those negative or embarrassing things that make for good examples or stories aren't always for sharing. You have to consider who will be affected your statements.

Dirty Dishes: Every Woman Has Them

Here are a few things to consider when speaking of others:
- Am I tarnishing someone's character?
- How does what I am saying make them feel?
- If someone was sharing my business, how would that make me feel?

In a lot of cases, when you are sharing your business with others, they keep their business private while passing judgment on you. Unfortunately, some women (myself included) have inherited the gossiping gene. We spend time commenting on others, when our sole purpose should be on ourselves.

Consider what kind of energy you're putting in the atmosphere; your goal should be to uplift others not put them down. Be mindful of the negative effects of gossiping the next time you attempt to dish out.

Dirty Dishes: Every Woman Has Them

Why is it so important to be mindful of how we speak in regard to others?

Dirty Dishes: Every Woman Has Them

Has anyone ever spoken unkindly to/or about you? How did that make you feel?

Dirty Dishes: Every Woman Has Them

Dirty Dishes: Every Woman Has Them

Gossip:
Mouths are moving; but nothing's being said.
Expressions of unbelief, watching necks in motion.
Eyes rolling, leaning closer to hear
Nothing of importance…
~Adrienne Latrise Draper~

Dirty Dishes: Every Woman Has Them

It's Not Polite to Talk and Chew!

How many times has your mother told you to close your mouth when you chew? Although she may have seemed petty at times, she was merely teaching you a life lesson-that it is very important to be aware of what goes into your mouth, as well as what comes out.

A lot of times as women, we simply talk too much. But it's not the fact that we are talking that is problematic; it is what we talk about that raises much concern.

Women have a tendency to share intimate and incriminating details about their relationship with friends and family members. But the problem is, while you've gotten over an issue and have forgiven your mate-your friends and family are still looking at the image you've illustrated to them. They eventually begin to resent your mate and have no remorse for expressing their disapproval or disdain for him.

While it is true that conflicts are inevitable, some conflicts can be avoided. You have to realize that sometimes a friend just wants you to listen. They do not need you to cosign or feed them negative energy. I reached a point where I had to be very selective with whom I shared my personal trials; and certain friends that only called to gossip or talk negatively about their mates-I ignored their calls altogether. As a friend, I am more interested in victories rather than misfortunes. It can become draining when someone is constantly complaining about his or her woes in life.

Consider the type of energy you're letting off into the atmosphere. Do you wake up angry? Or do you constantly express gratitude for your blessings? Do you condemn others often? Or are you known for complimenting people? You have to find some good in your life- even if it's just a little-and focus on it. Believe it

Dirty Dishes: Every Woman Has Them

or not, everyone has at least one thing they can complain about but everyone doesn't choose to speak on it.

I have no problem complimenting other women; I'd rather do that, than to point out their flaws. I am an observer by nature, so I can always find beauty in things. I am a very good listener and I'm careful to only say things that are uplifting and not offensive.

However, I am human and there are times when I'd rather just vent about my problems. It is during those moments where I write, or talk to God in the shower; you'd be surprised how he's able to give advice on how to handle things, even in the strangest places.

So the next time you feel the urge to speak with malice, think back to that old saying, "if you can't say anything nice, don't say anything at all;" and always remember what your mother taught you, "it's not polite to talk and chew!"

Dirty Dishes: Every Woman Has Them

How easy/difficult is it for you to speak kindly to/about others?

Dirty Dishes: Every Woman Has Them

It is important to get in the habit of using positive energy when speaking to others. When was the last time you complimented someone? How do you think that made them feel? How did you feel?

Dirty Dishes: Every Woman Has Them

Dirty Dishes: Every Woman Has Them

"The ultimate lesson all of us have to learn is unconditional love; which includes not only others but ourselves as well."

~Elisabeth Kübler-Ross~

Dirty Dishes: Every Woman Has Them

Keena's Deadly Recipe

My friend Keena had been sexually active ever since we were in grade school. In fact, she took the virginity of most of the boys at our school. As much as Keena performed sexual acts with our male classmates, it was older men that she thoroughly enjoyed being sexual with. As a teenager, she was always with men who had children our age.

I always wondered, "What happened to her to make her so sexual?" I later learned that participating in incest was pretty normal in her family. Being molested by uncles and cousins happened frequently at family gatherings because no one noticed when a few kids were missing. By the time she was old enough to realize it was wrong, it was too late. She had already been exposed to it and liked how it made her feel.

Keena had her share of diseases and unwanted pregnancies; but those frequent rapes that she experienced were considered justified by others who judged her by her promiscuous ways.

Keena had spiraled out of control and her deviant behavior was really beginning to have a negative effect on her life. Her family was embarrassed of her and constantly taunted her because of her poor personal hygiene. Even her mother shunned her and overlooked her daughters need to be loved and protected.

Since her family did little to support her; Keena spent most of her time living with random men, almost like a sex slave. Life for her became increasingly destructive and unfulfilling.

However, over time, Keena was introduced to someone who saw something greater in her. This individual was able to look past her flaws and

Dirty Dishes: Every Woman Has Them

imperfections and provide her with support and love. This person constantly reminded her that she doesn't have to look like what she's been through-and anytime she is ready to make a change in her life-she can.

    Keena had concocted a deadly recipe in her life; she was poisoning herself with fabricated ideas of what was right and what was wrong. Had she not been introduced to a master chef who demonstrated to her how to appropriately prepare her dish (her life)-she would have eventually been a victim of her own deadly recipe.

Dirty Dishes: Every Woman Has Them

Have you ever felt broken?

Dirty Dishes: Every Woman Has Them

Create steps you can take to heal from brokenness.

Step One: _____

Step Two: _____

Step Three: _____

Step Four: _____

Step Five: _____

Name three people in your life who can help you heal.

Person One: _____

Person Two: _____

Person Three: _____

*Share your thoughts with them and how you need their help!

Dirty Dishes: Every Woman Has Them

Dirty Dishes: Every Woman Has Them

"Our greatest illusion is to believe we are what we think ourselves to be."

~Henri Amiel~

Dirty Dishes: Every Woman Has Them

Fruit Dries Up!

Have you ever heard the saying, "Beauty is in the eyes of the beholder?" Often times I think about how God created so many varieties of people with distinct and unique differences. I think about how the things that make me who I am- are not the same elements that comprise who you are. Embracing your own natural beauty may be easier for some, and more difficult for others. But the truth is-in order to experience the fullness within you, you have to begin seeing yourself the way that God does.

At times, I like to dress fancy and add a little make-up to enhance my appearance; but with or without make-up, I am secure with me. Some women go out of their way to spend money they don't have in order to create a look, or a persona to feel good about them-selves. Their significance is validated by the clothing they wear or the cars they drive. But when they don't have the means to support their appearance/status, they lose it. Fortunately for me, I was taught beauty is within and I am made in the image of God.

On the contrary, there are some women who believe they are ugly. That statement may sound alarming, but it is true. Despite how often they are complimented, when they look in the mirror- all they see are their flaws. Although it is pretty typical for some women to criticize themselves- there are many women who never welcome praise at all. Instead of seeing their radiant eyes or smooth skin, they only see the scars and blemishes.

But I encourage you to look again. Look into the same mirror, through those same eyes and truly examine what you see. You have got to embrace your own beauty; we cannot expect to receive love from others to fill the void of our own self-love.

Dirty Dishes: Every Woman Has Them

Stop spending time focusing on your appearance, because as time progresses your appearance will change. It is no different than fruit that dries up; what were once juicy and ripe grapes will be dried up raisins if they are not eaten at the right time. Who you are should not be solely based on how you look; take the time to work on the inner you, because that's the part that truly matters in the end.

Dirty Dishes: Every Woman Has Them

When you consider the word, "UGLY," what thoughts come to mind? Is there any part of you that feels ugly or look ugly to you? Ugliness may mean different things to different people-but to me, it is a positive affirmation. When I see the word, "UGLY," I see an acronym that means:

U

Gotta

Love

Yourself

*So the next time you think "UGLY" embrace its new meaning.

■ ■

In many cases, we can turn negative thoughts into positive ones. How can you use the word, "FEAR" as a positive acronym? (Refer back to the word, "UGLY")

F _____

E _____

A _____

R _____

Use this space to take another negative word to turn into a positive acronym.

Dirty Dishes: Every Woman Has Them

"A man's face is his autobiography. A woman's face is her work of fiction"

~Oscar Wilde~

Dirty Dishes: Every Woman Has Them

Washing Dishes in Dirty Water

What does dishes look like that has been washed in dirty water you may ask? They look clean. We all know women or are women who may look like we have it together but are falling apart inside. We wear the mask so well sometimes people wouldn't know we are hurting because the signs aren't always visible. An unconscious learned behavior is when something is wrong don't show it. Some women are very much guarded and their privacy is respected.

You may have been raised in an environment where you felt invisible, and as an adult you make an effort to be acknowledged. Some women buy their friends as if it's a gym membership. They long for acceptance and at times over exert themselves by attending every function in fear of becoming invisible again.

Peniaphobia is the fear of poverty. Some women are obsessed with never returning to poverty, so they maintain a salary to be amongst the elite. Many also buy friends especially when they feel a friend has a bit of leverage over them. They want to prove they have just as much. If the two women are single you better believe she's going to present herself as being more attractive. If she were to have an unexpected expense she would panic. It's not that she can't afford to pay; it's the fear of other unexpected expenses so she'll go into overtime mode.

There are many other examples of appearing to have it all together but realistically living in a scattered state. Don't continue to consume yourself with fabrication. Halloween is the appropriate time to wear a mask not all year long. Accepting who you are creates a more authentic you!

Dirty Dishes: Every Woman Has Them

"A family divided against it-self, will perish together."
~Tamil Saying~

Dirty Dishes: Every Woman Has Them

Aluminum In The Microwave?

Rhonda and Keisha despised each other. As sisters, you would've thought they would be the best of friends; but actually, they rarely got along. Their parents had four children: Rhonda, Arthur, Keisha, and Sean. And since Rhonda was the oldest, she was naturally their mother's pride and joy. She was considered the "Pretty One" and there were pictures of her first steps, when she lost teeth as well as every birthday.

By the time Keisha was born, the only pictures of her childhood were from other relatives or taken at school. Her brother Arthur was great at sports so; you'd better believe you saw their mother at every game cheering him on from the sidelines. Sean took an interest in music; and as an adult, he performed as a local musician who opened up for national recording artists.

Keisha was the black sheep. Her mother never took an interest in what she was good at and always found fault in her. Rhonda naturally treated Keisha the same way because her mother taught them to taunt her. Arthur felt compelled to take Keisha under his wing; the love and support she lacked from their mother he provided.

When Keisha announced that she was engaged, there was no excitement from their mother. Her mother didn't help shop for the dress or the venue like she had done with Rhonda. At the wedding, Rhonda didn't smile in any pictures and when guests awed over Keisha and her husband, Rhonda made mention of how wonderful her husband was.

But over time, Rhonda and her husband had hit a rough spot. He couldn't take her alcoholism so he spent his evenings with other women. Keisha's relationship with her in-laws fit like a glove as opposed to Rhonda and her in-laws.

Dirty Dishes: Every Woman Has Them

Every attempt Keisha made to build a relationship with Rhonda was rejected. When their mother became ill, ironically, Keisha was the one who took care of her. Even on her deathbed, she preferred the care of Rhonda who was always unavailable. Keisha found it devastating how critical her mother was towards her in her last days and never understood why she hated her, so she asked. Her mother explained that she felt Keisha didn't need her. Keisha was smart and always-figured things out on her own; which made her mother feel worthless.

Keisha was able to get closure with her mother prior to her death; but as she tried to reconcile with her sister, she found it a daunting task. For Rhonda, it was difficult to treat Keisha any different from the way she was accustomed to.

Sometimes, we have to unlearn bad habits. In many cases, it means consciously reprogramming yourself to do better. Some people resist change because they fear losing control; but you have to take those necessary steps if you want to establish a better relationship.

What happens when you put aluminum in the microwave-it catches on fire, right? The same is true when we constantly feed negativity to others; eventually, relationships and friendships will become damaged beyond repair. Keisha's mother held the aluminum foil that caused her siblings and others to mistreat her. Think about your life; are you putting aluminum foil in someone's microwave? Is someone putting it in yours?

It is extremely important to live by the age old saying, "treat others how you want to be treated;" but unfortunately for Keisha and her siblings, their mother did not do such a great job instilling in them the right values-which ultimately, affected all of their relationships.

If you or someone you know shows characteristics

Dirty Dishes: Every Woman Has Them

of Keisha's mother or her sister Rhonda, it is time to make a change. You cannot continue going through life treating others unkindly; after all, your greatest rewards come by treating God's people with love and compassion.

Dirty Dishes: Every Woman Has Them

"Do not look where you fell, but where you slipped."
-African proverb-

Dirty Dishes: Every Woman Has Them

Addicted To The Flavor

Many people throughout the world battle with addiction; and it is important to note, drugs and alcohol are not the only things people become addicted to. Some people are addicted to lying, gambling, eating, violence, abuse, social media, pornography, etc. According to dictionary.com, addiction is the state of being enslaved to a habit, practice or to something that is psychologically or physically habit-forming.

There are many things that lead to addiction; but it is time to stop making excuses and work to break away from what could potentially be the death of you. You have my permission to break those dishes now. Whatever it is that has you enslaved is not healthy. Don't be ashamed of what you've done-be proud that you're not doing it anymore.

There are plenty of things that had me enslaved when my life was not on track. I put myself in dangerous situations, and if it were not for God on my side and many prayer warriors-I don't know where I would be right now. If you were anything like me, giving in to your addiction felt good at the time. It is like you become numb to the pain and detached from the reality of your situation. But when you are not consumed with your respective addiction, the pain is real; and you feel every ounce of it.

You just need to let go and let GOD! Every time you try to fix your problems alone-notice how it only causes more stress. The hardest thing to do is to believe in something you cannot see; but once you stop looking at how hard it is to have faith, you'll begin to see how easy GOD will work it out.

When I was away at college, my friends and I joined the choir. I remember singing a variety of songs in front of the student body every Thursday. On one

Dirty Dishes: Every Woman Has Them

Thursday, we sang a song that really caught my attention. It was Psalms 3. And to this day, whenever I experience life's challenges I reflect on that scripture:

^{1}Lord, how are they increased that trouble me! Many are they that rise up against me.

^{2}Many there be which say of my soul. There is no help for him in God. Selah.

^{3}But thou, O LORD, art a shield for me; my glory, and the lifter up of mine head.

^{4}I cried unto the LORD with my voice, and he heard me out of his holy hill. Selah.

^{5}I laid me down and slept; I awaked; for the LORD sustained me.

^{6}I will not be afraid of ten thousands of people that have set themselves against me round about.

^{7}Arise, O LORD; save me, O my God: for thou hast smitten all mine enemies upon the cheek bone; thou hast broken the teeth of the ungodly.

^{8}Salvation belongeth unto the LORD: thy blessing is upon thy people. Selah.

Dirty Dishes: Every Woman Has Them

Dirty Dishes: Every Woman Has Them

"There are wounds that never show on the body that are deeper and more hurtful than anything that bleeds."
~**Laurell K. Hamilton**~

Dirty Dishes: Every Woman Has Them

Everything Can't Be Slow-Cooked

I was a student ambassador for my college; and as an ambassador, I attended many conferences and workshops with other student government leaders throughout the country. I decided that summer school would help me achieve my goal of finishing college in four years, but something happened during my sophomore year that was totally unexpected; I became pregnant with my first child.

I panicked. So many emotions streamed through my veins. I thought about all the things I was working so hard to accomplish and how being a mother was not an ideal plan for me. I had to accept that I would soon be a mother-and a single mother at that.

One of the hardest things I had to do was tell my mother I was pregnant; but after she assured me that she would be supportive, I felt a huge weight lift from off me. It was not until my son was born that I became totally aware of my reality. Becoming a mother hit me like a ton of bricks. My life had transformed in the blink of an eye; I went from a four-year college to a community college and from renting my own apartment to residing in my childhood room again.

I never aspired to be a single mother; I dreamed of being a great wife. But like any obstacle in life you must adjust to it and find the blessing amidst the storm.

During the beginning stages of motherhood, I started crying uncontrollably and became very emotional. I don't even know why I was crying. One day, I was changing my son's diaper and my cousin asked me why I was crying; but I didn't know what to say.

Luckily, I was brave enough to seek medical help and was diagnosed with Post-Partum Depression. Post-

Dirty Dishes: Every Woman Has Them

Partum Depression is like an out-of-body experience. I couldn't control what was happening to me; and all I could do was, watch myself lose it. I had a lot of violent thoughts regarding my son that I personally wouldn't ever act on.

During that brief period of my life, several people stepped in to help me. I had a neighbor who would come and sit with me daily and I am forever grateful to her and others who never gave up on me.

Perhaps you are a woman who is experiencing some type of depression; I encourage you to share your thoughts with someone and get the help that you need. Depression can be overwhelming and it can creep up on you. A lot of women are afraid to admit they are experiencing signs of depression, and fear that people will think they are crazy. But you are not crazy-you may simply be dealing with a chemical imbalance.

Dirty Dishes: Every Woman Has Them

Dirty Dishes: Every Woman Has Them

"Only those who have helped themselves know how to help others, and to respect their right to help themselves."

~George Bernard Shaw~

Chapter 3:
Who's Washing Your Dishes?

It is a blessing when people volunteer to care for your child. Anytime you're in need of a sitter, they're just a phone call away. However, it is also imperative that you monitor who keeps your children, and how often they're not in your care.

If my child is spending more time at someone else's home, can I really expect for all of my rules to be implemented? There are so many mothers who chose careers that interfere with their home life, so the milestone moments are captured by other relatives or primary caregivers.

Some women take advantage of those caregivers; what starts off as you needing your child watched for a few hours have turned into an overnight sleepover. The occurrence happens so often, the caregivers, eventually expects to keep them for the weekend.

But there will come a time when those very people make themselves unavailable. That is when you need to re-evaluate your priorities. Your child is your responsibility. If you are the relative or friend who this has happened to-you need to demonstrate tough love. It's not ok for people to take advantage of you. I know you care for the well being of the child but the mother has to feel what others have felt when she didn't come back on time. These are her dishes!

Have you ever had an engagement at your home, and someone volunteered to wash the dishes? As they are washing the dishes, you notice that they don't wash as

Dirty Dishes: Every Woman Has Them

thoroughly as you do. That is why it is so essential that we handle our dishes (lives) with care and attention. Do not get comfortable letting others wash your dishes; otherwise, you will be stuck with extra grease and grime that you yourself would have gotten rid of.

Dirty Dishes: Every Woman Has Them

Why do you exhaust your resources for a sitter? Are you aware of the dangers if you were to send your children to multiple households? List your reasons for needing a sitter and number them in order of importance.

_____
_____
_____
_____
_____
_____
_____
_____
_____
_____
_____
_____
_____
_____
_____

Dirty Dishes: Every Woman Has Them

"Greed loses what it has gained"
~African Proverb~

Dirty Dishes: Every Woman Has Them

Full Course Meal

Many women are puzzled as to why he hasn't put a ring on it. They're checking off the checklist of what a healthy relationship consists of and in their mind they've passed the test. A man can look at all of the categories as side dishes simply because finances is his main course.

He can be physically attracted to her and her immaculate sense of style but her disregard to saving money may have made him re-evaluate a lifetime with her. Hypothetically, what if she stops working, or if business slows down for him, could they afford to continue this lifestyle twenty, ten or five years down the line? Financial maturity is essential in building a life with someone. It's okay to make large purchases in moderation but the obsession and entitlement to that lifestyle could be what's holding him back.

Women, who refuse to make those manageable adjustments, live their lives in replay as every successful man sees past the glitter and glam in search for a full course meal.

Dirty Dishes: Every Woman Has Them

"We have to dare to be ourselves, however frightening or strange that self may prove to be."

~May Sarton~

Dirty Dishes: Every Woman Has Them

Whose Recipe Are You Using?

More often than not, we as women find ourselves in relationships with people who cause us to alter who we are. We change how we dress; we embellish our lives and slowly begin living for our mate and not ourselves.

When Candice and Mike were dating, he would buy her expensive clothing and dress her up the way he saw fit. His recipe for her beauty consumed their lives. But everyone complimented her appearance-which made him feel like a proud chef.

Over the years, Candice became his little baby doll. But the more she implemented his recipe in her life, things that used to matter to her-slowly diminished. It wasn't long before she became a housewife. Her daily role was cooking, cleaning, and catering to him. And although Candice was raised not to shack, she found herself doing it anyway which haunted her.

Candice was losing so much of herself, she wanted to snap out of it, but she couldn't. Over time, she felt like a functioning addict and her ambitions were drowned out by what he needed of her.

Suddenly, several of her close friends noticed she changed. Candice became verbally abusive and distant towards others. Her words were like lyrical venom. But nothing was more intimidating than nonverbal. Her eyes spoke in sentences and spoke volumes about how she was feeling about herself and her current situation.

All in all, Candice was not happy with who she had become. As a child, she never imagined being a housewife and living through someone else's dreams and ambitions. She saw herself as a professional, a working- woman. But her family and friends felt that she should not complain; she had a man who was affluent and adored her. Candice did not have to pay bills, or go to work; in fact, her sole responsibility was taking care of home.

But that is not the recipe she concocted for her life. Candice allowed someone else to sabotage her recipe- which caused her to feel unimportant and voiceless.

In relationships, it is very common to feel like you don't have control over what is cooking in your oven, but there comes a time when you have to gather your own ingredients and your own supplies and confidently cook your own dish.

The only way to ensure that your dish (or your life) tastes the way you like it-is to simply cook it up yourself (now every once in a while, you can allow your mate to add a little sugar and spice-but remember ladies, you hold the measuring cup).

Dirty Dishes: Every Woman Has Them

Have you ever used someone else's recipe to cook? (In other words, have you ever allowed the influence of others to dictate how you live your life?) Discuss here.

Dirty Dishes: Every Woman Has Them

Is it possible to share your recipe (with your mate) and cook together? Or should you only use your own recipe and cook alone? Discuss here.

_____
_____
_____
_____
_____
_____
_____
_____
_____
_____
_____
_____
_____
_____
_____
_____
_____

Dirty Dishes: Every Woman Has Them

Dirty Dishes: Every Woman Has Them

"When dealing with people, let us remember we are not dealing with creatures of logic. We are dealing with creatures of emotion, creatures bristling with prejudices and motivated by pride and vanity."

~Dale Carnegie~

Dirty Dishes: Every Woman Has Them

Bad Cooks, Cook Bad!

Have you ever met someone who could not cook, but loved to share their cooking with others? They know their food is not tasty, but they'd rather make others suffer by eating it-than to refrain from cooking up disasters in the kitchen. It reminds me of an old saying, "Hurt People, Hurt People." Whether it is intentional or by chance-these people tend to impose on others what has been imposed on them.

It is important to quickly identify what makes you hurt others, because over time, relationships will get tarnished and family and friends will become distant in an effort to avoid major conflicts.

I had a really good friend that was so immersed in her hurtful past that she reflected that hurt onto me. I was so used to her behavior, that I simply viewed her outlandish attitude, as a personality trait-and did not take her antics personal.

At first, everyone noticed her bad attitude, but me. However, I eventually realized that my former friend never had anything positive to say. During our conversations, she was constantly challenging and ridiculing me. I would share personal moments with her, and she would share them with others. It was a bit difficult, but I had no choice but to no longer invest in that friendship.

There was no way I could continue clinging on to such a toxic relationship. I should have felt more comfortable talking with her, but every conversation became more and more awkward. I had to let go of her, before her behavior would start to make me act out of character. It was important for me to step away so that she could reevaluate why no one ever wanted to be around her.

Dirty Dishes: Every Woman Has Them

My former friend was a like a bad cook who wanted to force-feed others her burnt up dishes. If you have any bad cooks in your life: *boyfriends, husbands, girlfriends, wives, friends, etc.* let them eat their own food; it is time to take control over what you will and will not eat-and remember, "Bad Cooks, Cook Bad," so leave them in their own kitchen and make your way back to yours.

Dirty Dishes: Every Woman Has Them

Are there any bad cooks in your life? (In other words, are there any negative people in your life right now that are stunting your growth?)

Dirty Dishes: Every Woman Has Them

How do you deal with bad cooks in your life? What actions can you take to eliminate them from your kitchen?

Dirty Dishes: Every Woman Has Them

Dirty Dishes: Every Woman Has Them

Never be mentored by someone who missed their moment because they will molest you with their jealousy.
~Bishop T. D. Jakes~

Dirty Dishes: Every Woman Has Them

Who's Cooking in your Kitchen?

It is very essential that you have control over who is cooking in your kitchen-or rather-who is feeding your mind, body and soul. Do you have individuals around you that nourish you and fulfill you; or do you have people who feed you lies, deception, and envious agendas? Women, I encourage you to go into your kitchen-to that deepest part of your soul and put everyone out whose intentions are not to enhance your life and help you to grow.

Obviously, there are individuals in your life that do not want to see you succeed at all. Like crabs in a barrel, they would rather pull you down to where they are, than to lend a hand and support your victories. But whatever you do, do not be deceived by their pretentious support for you. Take control of your life by acknowledging that there is no need for those who do not sustain you. Reflect on these scenarios below, and if you have individuals in your life who have deposited these messages in your being-**GET THEM OUT OF YOUR KITCHEN!**

- You have saved money and feel it is time to invest in a house. **Their response is**: *it is great you have saved for a house, but an apartment is better; if something goes wrong, at least your landlord is responsible for getting it fixed.*

- You are talking about taking a cruise with some girlfriends. **Their response is:** *that sounds like fun, even though it is a bit dangerous; what if it hits an iceberg?*

- One of your favorite comedians is coming to town and you are talking about getting tickets to the concert. **Their response is:** *he did not get a good review in the last city, are you sure you want to waste your money?*

Dirty Dishes: Every Woman Has Them

- You are hosting an event. **Their response is**: *the place looks amazing and you have put a lot of money into your event, are you sure you are going to have a big turnout?*

- You are getting work done on your house. **Their response is:** *it looks like everything is coming along; I personally would have let it burn to the ground and used the insurance money to get a new one.*

- You are in college. **Their response is:** *I am glad you are bettering your education, but when are you going to finish? My friends' kids are doctors and lawyers and you are all the same age.*

Dirty Dishes: Every Woman Has Them

Add your own scenario:

_____

_____

_____

_____

Their response is

_____

_____

_____

_____

Add your own scenario:

_____

_____

_____

_____

Their response is

_____

_____

_____

_____

Dirty Dishes: Every Woman Has Them

Add your own scenario:

_____
_____
_____
_____

Their response is

_____
_____
_____
_____

Add your own scenario:

_____
_____
_____
_____

Their response is

_____
_____
_____
_____

Dirty Dishes: Every Woman Has Them

Dirty Dishes: Every Woman Has Them

"We have all heard the story of the animal standing in doubt between two stacks of hay and starving to death."

~Abraham Lincoln~

Dirty Dishes: Every Woman Has Them

Should I Try this Dish?

Have you ever been out with someone, became extremely hungry and decided to go get something to eat; but while in route, the other person asks you, "what do you want to eat," and you respond, "It doesn't matter." Or perhaps, your husband or boyfriend comes home and wants to take you out for the evening and asks, "Where would you like to go," and again you reply, "It doesn't matter." Can you imagine how annoying being indecisive is to others?

It was always hard for me to make decisions- even simple ones. I spent most of my life thinking that I would experience less conflict if I simply allowed others to make decisions for me. I never viewed my indecisiveness as a weakness-I figured if someone else made the decisions, they couldn't fault me if they didn't like what was decided.

However, what I never anticipated was that in addition to people seeing my indecisiveness as a weakness- that they would also see me as too passive to control my own life. I realized that the more I allowed others to make decisions for my life, the more they believed they were entitled to control my life. My freedom was unwillingly given to my family and close ones-all because I had allowed them to make decisions for me.

I really had a difficult time managing between being a loyal wife and a loyal daughter. Growing up in a large, closely knit family, meant constantly being invited to Sunday dinners, church functions, birthday parties, retirement parties and so on; but my husband could not understand my obligation to my family. He grew up with a smaller family that did not gather as often as mine. Therefore, I had to constantly decide who I should please- my family (who I've known all my life) or my husband- (who I was building a new life with). There were times

Dirty Dishes: Every Woman Has Them

when my husband felt I should have just married my family. He did not feel he was getting the attention he needed from me because I was constantly running errands and being attentive to my family. On the other hand, when I would cut down on spending time with my family, they felt as though my husband was changing me. I could not win for losing.

As a mother of four, I became really stressed out trying to appease both my family and my husband's family during the holidays. Everyone wanted me to bring my children over, but that meant visiting at least three homes-which became very overwhelming. I felt that no one took me seriously. Until I could make my own decisions and stand firmly on those decisions-they would always only see me as a laid back, passive woman.

Have you ever tried a dish that someone else prepared and instantly you said to yourself, "they've added too many ingredients?" Well, I was just like that dish with too many ingredients, prepared by someone else. My family and my husband were not capable of properly preparing my dish (my life) because I was the only one who knew what and how many ingredients to use.

Sometimes, we allow people to eat away at us like our lives are their buffet; and as long as you allow people to freely make decisions for you, or undermine your choices you will never be truly fulfilled.

Dirty Dishes: Every Woman Has Them

Dirty Dishes: Every Woman Has Them

"To serve is beautiful; but only if it is done with joy, a whole heart and a free mind."

~Pearl S. Buck~

Dirty Dishes: Every Woman Has Them

Mothers Are The Best Cooks

Mona was a 22 year-old new mother who still lived at home with her parents. She came from a very small family; and caring for a newborn was a learning experience for her. Her mother would constantly correct her on the proper way to change the baby, hold the baby, play with the baby, and teach the baby. But when Mona became comfortable caring for her daughter, her mother continued to add her expertise.

Over time, Mona felt less like a mother and more like a sibling to her child. As her daughter had gotten older, Mona began to be a bit firmer with her mother-but her rearing practices were always rejected. This caused a major divide in their relationship. Arguing became their number one way of communicating. And though Mona knew it was not right to disrespect her mother, she needed her mother to know that she was the parent of her child.

Anytime Mona said, "no," to her daughter, Mona's mother would tell her, "yes". That taught Mona's daughter that if she wants something, just ask grandma.

Grandmothers, I know your intentions are merely to assist-but your role as grandmother does not require you to be controlling and dismissive. Ask yourself; did your mother raise your children? Are you repeating some of the same behaviors that were imposed upon you? It is important for you and your daughter to have a respectable relationship because children pick up on tension.

Respect your daughter's role as mother while you enjoy your role as grandmother. Be an aid to your daughter-but only when she says she needs it.

Dirty Dishes: Every Woman Has Them

Has your mother (or guardian) every over-stepped her boundary in your life? How did that make you feel?

_____
_____
_____
_____
_____
_____
_____
_____
_____
_____
_____
_____
_____
_____
_____
_____
_____

Dirty Dishes: Every Woman Has Them

There is a saying, "Mother Knows Best." Do you believe that statement to be true? Why or why not.

_____
_____
_____
_____
_____
_____
_____
_____
_____
_____
_____
_____
_____
_____
_____
_____

Dirty Dishes: Every Woman Has Them

"Parents...are sometimes a bit of a disappointment to their children. They don't fulfill the promise of their early years."

~Anthony Powell~

Dirty Dishes: Every Woman Has Them

Teaching Mama How To Cook!

Over the years, the role of parenting has shifted. There are so many instances where children are practically raising their parents. Instead of their child participating in high school activities he/she has to care for younger siblings or work to help with bills. It becomes a strain when those children become adults that assume the same responsibility in regard to their parents.

It isn't a case where the parent is disabled or unable to care for him or herself; the parent just decided that early on, he/she would pour their responsibilities on to their child (ren). It is not fair to put your child in that predicament; children are taught to honor thy mother and thy father so they would feel guilty if they did not subscribe to their parent's commands?

The problem with parents who over-step their boundaries by forcing their children to practically raise them; is that, when their children become adults it will be difficult for them to sustain healthy relationships with their mates because of their obligation to their parent.

Parents are supposed to teach their children how to cook. But there are way too many children in the kitchen, when they should be outside playing. If you are a parent who allows your child to assume your responsibilities, STOP.

Perhaps your parent treated you the same way and you don't know how to handle your child (ren) appropriately; in that case, seek outside assistance. You do not want your child to grow up despising you or more importantly, imposing the same jaded behaviors on their own children.

Dirty Dishes: Every Woman Has Them

"Being considered or labeled mentally disordered-abnormal, crazy, mad, psychotic, sick, it matters not what variant is used-is the most profoundly discrediting classification that can be imposed on a person today."

~Thomas S. Szasz~

Dirty Dishes: Every Woman Has Them

Fine China

My son did all the things a child his age was supposed to do; but at a very young age, I noticed there was a problem with his speech. After discussing my concerns with his doctor and teachers, I was told that he was fine and his speech would improve over time. A few years later, he was diagnosed with Intellectual Disability (the new term for Mental Retardation) and Sound System Disorder.

When I first received the news, I was devastated; I thought about all of the stigmas associated with the term and immediately felt sadness for my son. I thought back to grammar school; and how my peers made fun of retarded kids and made life pretty difficult for them. I did not want others to look at him differently or treat him unkind because of his condition. I wanted people to see my son the way that I did-as perfectly fine.

Eventually, I had to accept that my son had this condition and the best thing to do was to link him to the resources that could help him. I had to realize it was not about me, but about him. I became an instant advocate for him and we experienced many hardships along the way. He was discriminated against by educators and family members. It broke my heart to see others lack compassion for my child. But I did not give up; I continued researching, praying, and seeking advice all in an effort to assist my son.

My son is a true example of the best friend anyone could ever have. He's compassionate, intelligent, witty,

Dirty Dishes: Every Woman Has Them

and supportive; but it is his smile that will soften the coldest heart. My son reminds me of fine china. Fine china is beautiful and warms the hearts of many but it must always be handled with care and delicacy.

Often times, we are misinformed about various types of mental illnesses and disorders; so naturally, our lack of information can result in us placing judgment upon others. However, it is never justified to treat people cruelly or unkind. Take a moment to consider how you treat people. Do you toss them around like broken dishes, or treat them like the fine china that you bring out for special occasions? You must remember, everyone deserves to be treated with respect, decency and most importantly, with love.

Dirty Dishes: Every Woman Has Them

Have you ever been treated differently because of your uniqueness?

Dirty Dishes: Every Woman Has Them

Have you ever treated someone unkind due to his or her disability?

_____

_____

_____

_____

_____

_____

_____

_____

_____

_____

_____

_____

_____

_____

_____

_____

_____

Dirty Dishes: Every Woman Has Them

Dirty Dishes: Every Woman Has Them

"We cannot make it rain, but we can see to it that the rain falls on prepared soil."

~Henri J. M. Nouwen~

Chapter 4:

How To Clean Your Dishes

Sometimes, the most challenging thing we as women must do is acknowledge and accept our dirty dishes (our flaws, insecurities, weaknesses, issues, etc.). We tend to work so diligently at trying to be the best versions of ourselves, but are constantly reminded of the stench coming from our kitchen. On a good note, there are tons of ways we can begin washing those dirty dishes.

I remember as a child I was given weekly chores; my siblings and I had to ensure that our house was clean from top to bottom. Each week, we had to alternate between who cleaned the kitchen, the bathroom and the living room.

I always found that cleaning the kitchen was the most time consuming. You had to clean the refrigerator, the stove, the table, the counters, sweep and mop the floor and most importantly, wash the dirty dishes. And although we had a dishwasher, sometimes, there were pots and pans that needed to be scrubbed and cleaned by hand.

But there was nothing like the joy on my mother's face when she came home to a clean house. Imagine how you would feel walking into a spotless kitchen where you

Dirty Dishes: Every Woman Has Them

could practically eat off the floor. Having a clean kitchen is like having a more refined you.

Can you imagine how your loved ones would feel to experience a more refined you? What are you willing to sacrifice to make that happen?

There is no perfect way to clean your dishes; but you must follow some type of process. You cannot dry your dishes before they are rinsed. It is important to truly examine your dirty dishes to make sure you are addressing all of the tough spots. All in all, if you do not take the time to carefully wash, rinse and dry your dishes-you kitchen (life) will never be in order.

Dirty Dishes: Every Woman Has Them

"A friend is a second self."

~Aristotle~

Dirty Dishes: Every Woman Has Them

Preheat Your Stove!

  Enjoying a delicious meal is like celebrating a healthy relationship; your body is edified, you feel good and more than likely, you want to savor every moment of the experience. Typically, when preparing meals, there are some essential steps you must take to ensure your meal will be prepared properly and to your satisfaction (boiling your water, preheating your stove, etc.) and the same is true with relationships. In order to ensure that you get the best out of your relationship, you and your mate should be friends first.

  It may seem cliché to advise forming a friendship before committing to a relationship, but in doing so you can prevent a number of unnecessary conflicts in the future. The moment people get too comfortable with their mate, one or the other starts to change. If you and your mate were not friends first, communicating your wants and needs could possibly be a bit more complicated.

  But becoming friends first allows you and your mate to establish a more solid and trustworthy relationship. Friends are able to share nearly everything, even embarrassing moments. Friends tend to avoid putting you in compromising situations and always have your best interest in mind. For the most part, a mate who is also considered a friend will take your happiness just as seriously as their own.

  There was a guy who I dated who constantly placed my feelings and desires on the backburner; and before I knew it I was accepting a lot of negative behaviors from him that I would have never settled for. Trying to maintain that relationship became a daunting task. I remember one day he told me, "I don't respect you!" And although I was totally shocked, I was also relieved. I saw myself changing

Dirty Dishes: Every Woman Has Them

to adapt to him but I received little attention and affection from him throughout the relationship.

That relationship taught me a huge lesson about investing in people who I do not consider friends first. A true friend would have never taken advantage of everything that I gave him so freely. Although he had some great qualities, it became evident that he and I were not equally yoked.

In addition to becoming friends with your mate first, it is also important that your mate is compatible with your children. Often times someone can be really interested in investing in you, but detest your children. You must question to yourself, "How can we establish a healthy relationship if this person and my children do not have a good rapport?" While it is not the decision of your children whom you date, their feelings should be important when you are selecting a mate. There are some women who want a relationship so bad, that they do not consider the feelings of their children; but in the future, that stance will have a detrimental effect on you and your child's relationship.

Remember women; it is not healthy to expose your children to someone who may be temporarily in your life. In other words, take the time to preheat your stove; it will save you from having to deal with unnecessary issues or drama within your relationship.

Dirty Dishes: Every Woman Has Them

Dirty Dishes: Every Woman Has Them

You have many choices. You can choose forgiveness over revenge, joy over despair. You can choose action over apathy.... You hold the key to how well you make the emotional adjustment to your divorce and consequently how well your children will adapt.
~Stephanie Marston~

Dirty Dishes: Every Woman Has Them

Change The Temperature

My mother did everything she could to make up for what my biological father didn't do. I respect the fact that she never spoke negatively about him, despite his many broken promises and instability throughout my life. As a mother, she did not ever complain.

My mother was always wise beyond her years; and even if my siblings and I disagreed with her and her instruction-we always knew in our hearts that she was coming from a loving place.

Throughout my childhood, my mother took us on many family trips; and I was always thrilled to be around so many extended relatives. Many of my friends assumed we were wealthy because of everything they witnessed my mother do for us.

It always meant a lot to me to please my mother; but when I became pregnant with my first child, I just knew she would be extremely disappointed in me. I felt as though I had made the very mistake she tried so hard to shield me from. To my surprise, she did not judge me; she simply did what any loving mother would do- supported and helped me through my pregnancy.

I was a single mother and like so many others I had to make a lot of sacrifices. I didn't carry the weight of resentment because my mother didn't. We made the most of our situation; which eliminated the drama of two colliding egos.

My husband and I try to instill the same morals and values we acquired as children. Since we both experienced going from a two- parent household to single parent households, we understood what we needed to do to keep it healthy and make it work. It's so easy to get caught up in

Dirty Dishes: Every Woman Has Them

your own emotions, but when you have children, the best example to give them is how to let go and let God.

When parenting, you have to relieve yourself of the pain that comes from failed relationships. Children deserve to get the best from their parents; and finding a common ground is imperative to your children's mental stability.

Changing the temperature allows you to experience warmth and coolness; and the same is true with parenting; changing the way you treat one another makes a huge difference in the rearing of your child. So don't be selfish; begin making the necessary adjustments to ensure your child gets your very best.

Dirty Dishes: Every Woman Has Them

Is your relationship with your child/ren's father healthy? What steps should you take towards letting go finding a common ground?

_____

_____

_____

_____

_____

_____

_____

_____

_____

_____

_____

_____

_____

_____

_____

Dirty Dishes: Every Woman Has Them

"The most assiduous task of parenting is to define the difference between boundaries and bondage."

~Barbara Kingsoliver~

Dirty Dishes: Every Woman Has Them

Cook in Your Own Kitchen!

Mothers do not stop being mothers when their child turns eighteen. If their child is ever in need whether it is for financial or moral support, real mothers make themselves available. But there are times when mothers can over step their boundaries; especially when it comes to freely sharing their disdain for their child's chosen mate.

While mothers have a right to their own opinion, it is important for them to remember that they cannot live life for their child. Your son or daughter has to do the same thing you did-feel out the world and learn through his or her own experiences. Unfortunately, you cannot protect them from everything; and you certainly cannot run interference in their household either.

Remember, times have changed; in today's society, there are very few arranged marriages. So the choices your son and daughters make regarding their mates should be respected. Learn to love and accept your son or daughter-in law because if they have children, their children will notice how you treat both of their parents. Therefore, to avoid tension and any disconnection within your family, I urge you to simply cook in your own kitchen.

Cooking in your own kitchen will require you putting your ego aside and staying in your own lane. Offering to cook a dish (or giving your opinion) is fine; but coming into someone's kitchen and preparing a feast without their consent or against their will is not only rude but could prove to be very offensive.

Dirty Dishes: Every Woman Has Them

Has someone ever tried to take over in your kitchen (have control in your life)? Name the person, and discuss how you will/did reclaim your own power.

Dirty Dishes: Every Woman Has Them

Dirty Dishes: Every Woman Has Them

There are several steps you can take to begin washing your dishes (or cleaning up your life). The next few pages will discuss four main areas to consider: *Health, Education, Parenting and Spirituality.*

Health:

As women, our health is very important. We cannot cheat ourselves out of a healthy life. Any pains or irregular symptoms shouldn't go unseen. Communicate with your physician. It's not acceptable to put off doctor visits in fear of bad results.

If your family has a history of heart disease, take the necessary steps toward prevention. If your family has a history of hypertension, use less salt and control your stressors. If your family has a history of cancer, communicate with your physician so if additional testing is needed so you can catch it early if it happens. If you are borderline diabetic, do exactly what your physician says to avoid diabetes.

If you have a precondition, follow the proper instructions from your physician to avoid hospitalization. When doctors prescribe medication, rarely your condition is it temporary. You don't want to pop pills for the rest of your life; nor do you want your loved ones to be affected by it all. I love you and your family loves you too; and we want to see you be healthy.

Dirty Dishes: Every Woman Has Them

Education:

Even as a single mother, pursuing my education meant everything to me. I knew very early on that being a woman requires being self-assured, grounded and educated. As a mother of four, I was pregnant three times while I attended college. It was not easy; but I was determined to accomplish my academic pursuits.

I attended an institution in Knoxville, Tennessee many years ago; and while I was there, I remember hearing a sermon that changed my life. Pastor James H. Davis explained how many people want to turn around when they reach their midpoint (because that's when things seem to get harder and harder); but in actuality, the same distance forward is the same if you turn around so it would behoove you to keep moving forward.

I did move forward; and eventually, I received my undergraduate degree. Despite the trials that you may encounter while pursuing your education/dreams (such as financial, academic, etc.) never give up. There are many resources and assistance programs available to you; but you must be diligent and pro-active in order to find them.

Education is something that no one can ever take away from you; so with everything that you have, continue to invest in the learning process.

Parenting:

Dirty Dishes talks a lot about parenting because those relationships are the ones that truly shape who we are. If you were abandoned by your parents, or were abused by your parents, chances are you have a lot of unresolved hurt built up inside. However, if your parents nurtured you and praised your achievements, there is a chance you possess great morals and values and find forgiveness to be an art.

It is very essential to be unique and innovative with your parenting styles. You must remember that each of your children are different; and, require different needs from you. If you have any concerns about your parenting, seeking professional guidance. Children are supposed to look up to their parents. And although parents are not perfect, they are the first teachers.

If you are someone's child, always show respect and gratitude towards your parents. Even if your parent(s) raised you poorly, at the end of the day they helped to bring you into existence. And that, in and of itself, is a true blessing.

Dirty Dishes: Every Woman Has Them

Spirituality:

When you lose sight of who you are and who you belong to-you run the risk of being held captive by forces beyond your control. There were several moments in my life where I lost control; but I had to reconnect with a higher being and become the woman my children and loved ones needed me to be. I used to be a people pleaser; but now I am fully content with pleasing God. When I lost dear friends, experienced failed relationships, and struggled with my career goals-all I could do was turn to God.

Perhaps you call God "Allah," "Buddha," "Yahweh" or "Jah;" at the end of the day- aligning yourself with a being higher than you is the key to your success.

You may not know how to wash your dirty dishes, or how to get bad cooks out of your kitchen; but I assure you, if you were to turn to the Ultimate Chef (God) and trust him with your kitchen (your life) then and only then, will you truly be fulfilled.

Dirty Dishes: Every Woman Has Them

As you may have noticed throughout, "Dirty Dishes," there is a quote to open up each section. Listed below are a few more affirming quotes that women can reflect on daily:

****

"If I do not define myself, for myself, then I will be crunched into other people's fantasies of me and eaten alive."

~Audre Lorde~

■ ■

"Women must not accept; she must challenge. She must not be awed by that which has been built up around her; she must reverence that woman in her which struggles for expression."

~Maragret Sanger~

■ ■

"When a woman tells the truth, she is creating the possibility for more truth around her."

~Adrienne Rich~

■ ■

Dirty Dishes: Every Woman Has Them

Do you have any favorite quotes, scriptures, sayings, etc.? If so, state them here. Using quotes in our everyday lives can be very liberating and life changing.

Quote/Scripture/Saying:

_____
_____
_____
_____

Quote/Scripture/Saying:

_____
_____
_____
_____

Quote/Scripture/Saying:

_____
_____
_____
_____

Quote/Scripture/Saying:

_____
_____
_____
_____

Quote/Scripture/Saying:

_____
_____
_____
_____

Dirty Dishes: Every Woman Has Them

List the steps you need to take to stop letting your dishes soak:

Step 1:

Step 2:

Step 3:

List the "bad cooks" that need to get out of your kitchen

Bad Cook # 1:

Bad Cook # 2:

Bad Cook # 3:

What commitments will you make to keep your dishes clean?

Commitment # 1:

Commitment # 2:

Commitment #3:

Dirty Dishes: Every Woman Has Them

After reading, "Dirty Dishes," have you identified any dishes that need to be cleaned in your kitchen? Discuss.

Made in the USA
Charleston, SC
11 February 2013